The Modern Snare Drummer

by Ron Spagnardi

Design and Layout by Scott Bienstock
Cover Photo by Jim Esposito

Published by
Modern Drummer Publications, Inc.
12 Old Bridge Road
Cedar Grove, NJ 07009 USA

INTRODUCTION

The Modern Snare Drummer offers a collection of thirty-eight solos for the intermediate to advanced student of drumming. Designed to challenge both technical and reading skills, these solos should be practiced regularly and diligently to achieve the desired end result.

Each of the thirty-eight solos is preceded by a Solo Analysis page containing a brief explanation of the solo's structure and highlights, with an emphasis on the more difficult sections of the piece. The Practice Measures on the same page are selected bars that may present a reading or execution challenge. It is suggested that you practice and master these before moving on to the solo.

Page 4 of the book contains 30 Preparatory Exercises, which can be used as a daily warm-up prior to practicing the solos. Nearly all of the exercises presented are used in some manner within the solos, and mastery of these patterns will help ensure accurate performance of the thirty-eight solo pieces.

Suggested stickings are presented on many occasions throughout the book. When a recommended sticking is not indicated, alternate sticking leading with the right hand (for right-handed players) will generally work best. The choice of sticking is often a matter of personal preference, so feel free to experiment with optional stickings wherever applicable.

An assortment of time signatures ranging from 2/4 to 12/8 is applied throughout this text. It Is strongly recommended that you play each solo slowly at first, striving for accuracy and technical fluency. Be sure to practice these solos with a metronome, bearing in mind that the metronome markings are simply suggested tempos. All of the solos can be performed slower or faster than suggested, depending on your reading and technical skills. The guidance of a competent instructor is always highly recommended.

CONTENTS

	PAGE
Introduction	3
30 Preparatory Exercises	4
Solo 1 In 2/4	7
Solo 2 In 3/8	9
Solo 3 In 9/8	11
Solo 4 In 3/4	13
Solo 5 In 6/8	15
Solo 6 In 5/4	17
Solo 7 In 7/8	19
Solo 8 In 2/4	21
Solo 9 In 3/8	23
Solo 10 In 4/4	25
Solo 11 In 5/8	27
Solo 12 In 3/4	29
Solo 13 In 6/8	31
Solo 14 In 5/4	33
Solo 15 In 7/8	35
Solo 16 In 3/8	37
Solo 17 In 2/4	39
Solo 18 In 12/8	41
Solo 19 In 4/4	43
Solo 20 In 7/8	45
Solo 21 In 5/8	47
Solo 22 In 3/4	49
Solo 23 In 6/8	51
Solo 24 In 5/4	53
Solo 25 In 4/4	55
Solo 26 In 3/8	57
Solo 27 In 2/4	59
Solo 28 In 9/8	61
Solo 29 In 4/4	63
Solo 30 In 5/8	65
Solo 31 In 3/4	67
Solo 32 In 6/8	69
Solo 33 In 2/4	71
Solo 34 In 3/8	73
Solo 35 In 5/4	75
Solo 36 In 6/8	77
Solo 37 In 4/4	79
Solo 38 In 12/8	81

30 PREPARATORY EXERCISES

These exercises can be used as warm-up material for the solos in this book. Most of the patterns here are used in one manner or another within the solos. Mastery of these exercises will help you build the necessary speed, stamina, endurance, and control to successfully perform the material that follows.

Repeat each exercise fifteen to twenty times at different tempos, with rolls and rudiments played both open and closed. Be sure to reverse the sticking where indicated.

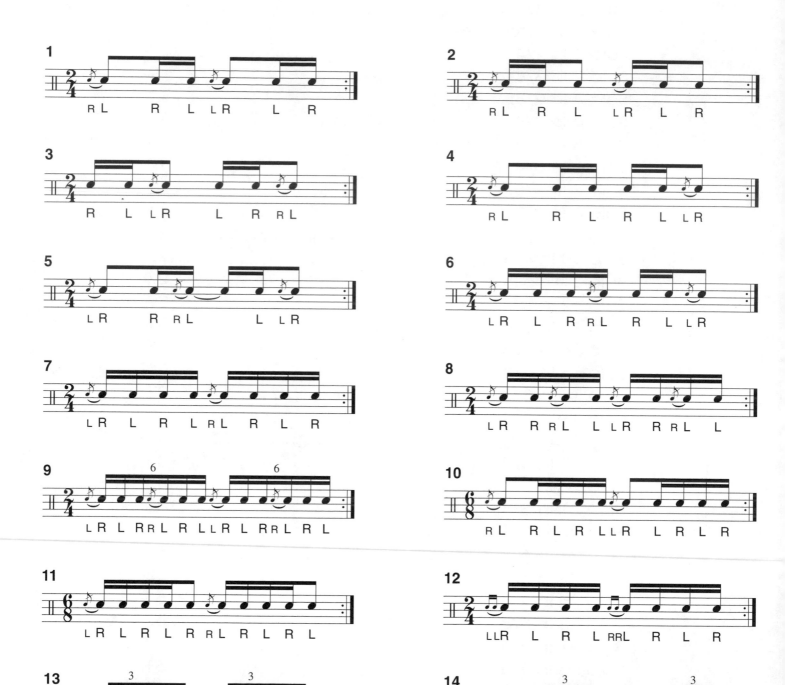

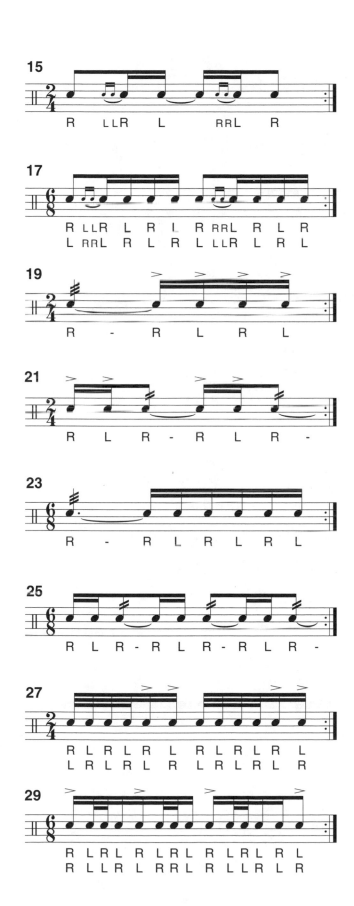
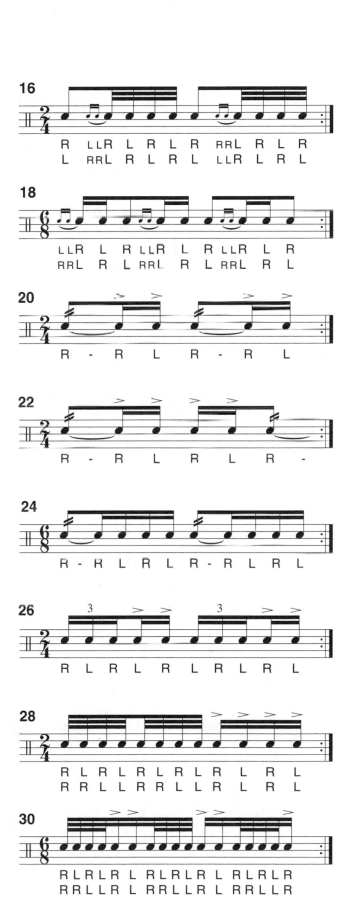

SOLO 1 ANALYSIS

This first solo is a simple piece in 2/4 in the marching band style, and should be performed at M.M. = 126 or faster. A mixture of accents, flams, and short rolls combine to make this opening piece a challenging one at faster tempos. Start slowly and gradually build to 126 bpm. Reading accuracy is always first and foremost in importance.

PRACTICE MEASURES

Measures 11–12
Pay careful attention to the accent phrasing here.

Measures 29–30
Back-to-back flams can sometimes present problems at faster tempos.

Measures 33–34
Flams and short rolls give this phrase an across-the-barline feel.

SOLO 1

SOLO 2 ANALYSIS

At an M.M. of dotted quarter note = 72, the following solo in 3/8 is actually played with a "one" feel. Flams and drags leading into 16th-note and 16th-note-triplet figures are used often here. The short rolls work best as five-stroke rolls with an accent on the final stroke.

PRACTICE MEASURES

Measure 14
Flam taps need to be executed with precise rhythmic accuracy.

Measures 21–22
Watch the accents and drags in this two-bar triplet phrase.

Measures 37–38
Accenting the first stroke of the five-stroke roll is an interesting contrast to the usual five-stroke roll with an accent on the last note.

SOLO 2

SOLO 3 ANALYSIS

Solo 3 is in 9/8 time, and though it may appear complex at first glance, 9/8 is simply an extension of 3/8 and 6/8. It can be counted in "nine," or as three groups of 3/8. Rolls, rudiments, accents, and a few polyrhythmic phrases make this an interesting piece to perform.

PRACTICE MEASURES

Measures 13–15
This three-bar phrase may require some extra emphasis prior to attempting the entire solo.

Measure 25
The rolls in this measure must be played softer so as to achieve a distinct contrast between the rolls and the accents.

Measures 30–32
The accent pattern in the final three bars of Solo 3 need to be balanced correctly against the non-accented notes.

SOLO 3

SOLO 4 ANALYSIS

The following 3/4 solo at quarter note = 108 offers a challenge to hand and eye. Take it slowly, and gradually work up to the suggested tempo. Pay careful attention to the accented 16th notes used throughout the solo. (See the Practice Measures below.) Practice this solo with a metronome to ensure a steady tempo, and focus on crisp execution of all the figures.

PRACTICE MEASURES

Measures 13–15
This three-bar, 16th-note phrase requires control and concentration.

Measure 31
More accented 16th-note figures occur in bar 31.

Measures 37–39
This three-bar phrase contains some tricky accent placement and short-roll combinations.

SOLO 4

SOLO 5 ANALYSIS

Solo 5, which is in 6/8, starts out simply but increases in complexity as you proceed. Play the Practice Measures slower than M.M. = 76 for starters. This solo also has an assortment of various-length rolls—from press rolls to dotted quarter and dotted half notes. Don't overlook the importance of accuracy in the execution of these rolls.

PRACTICE MEASURES

Measures 17–18
The accents add flavor to this basic two-bar passage.

Measures 25–27
Note the dotted 8th note followed by a dotted 8th-note roll in every bar below.
Count out this three-bar section and sing the pattern aloud if necessary.

Measures 43–44
This two-bar passage features press rolls in measure 44. The press roll is simply a flammed buzz stroke.

SOLO 5

SOLO 6 ANALYSIS

Solo 6 is in 5/4, but it has a strong, syncopated swing feel. For the best effect, all of the accents should stand out above the non-accented notes. This solo can be performed two ways: first with straight 8th notes, and then with 8th notes with a jazz conception.

PRACTICE MEASURES

Measures 7–9
Be cautious of the accents in bar 9.

Measures 16–17
Eighth notes and quarter notes tied to downbeats place heavy emphasis on the offbeats in this phrase.

Measures 29–30
Two consecutive bars of accented triplets can be quite dynamic. Notice the quarter-note triplet created by the accents on beats 3, 4, and 5 of the second bar.

R L R L R L R L R L R L R L R   L R L R L R L R L R L R L R L R
pp   *p*   *mp*   *mf*

SOLO 6

SOLO 7 ANALYSIS

The next solo is a venture into 7/8. Counting up to "seven" in 7/8 time can be awkward and difficult. It's much easier to count seven in the same manner in which the figures are written in the solo: 1,2,3—1,2,3,4. Don't increase the tempo here until you feel relaxed and comfortable playing in 7/8.

PRACTICE MEASURES

Measures 10–11

The sticking in this two-bar phrase can be played several ways. Single sticking will put the accents on alternate hands. (See A below.) A sticking pattern of RLL on the triplets keeps all the accents on the right hand. (See B below.) Left-handed players should try LRR on the triplets.

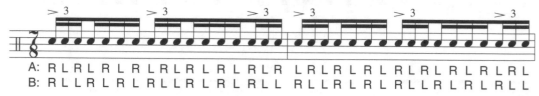

A: R L R L R L R L R L R L R L R L R L R   L R L R L R L R L R L R L R L R L R L
B: R L L R L R L R L L R L R L R L L   R L L R L R L R L R L L R L R L R L L

Measures 19–21

This heavily accented three-bar section may be one of the most difficult to play in the entire solo.

R L R L R L R L R L R L R L   R L R L R L R L R L R L R L R L   R L R L R L R L R L R L R L R L R
f   *ff*

Measures 25–26

These two bars require very careful counting.

L R R   L R R L R   L R L L R L R L R

SOLO 7

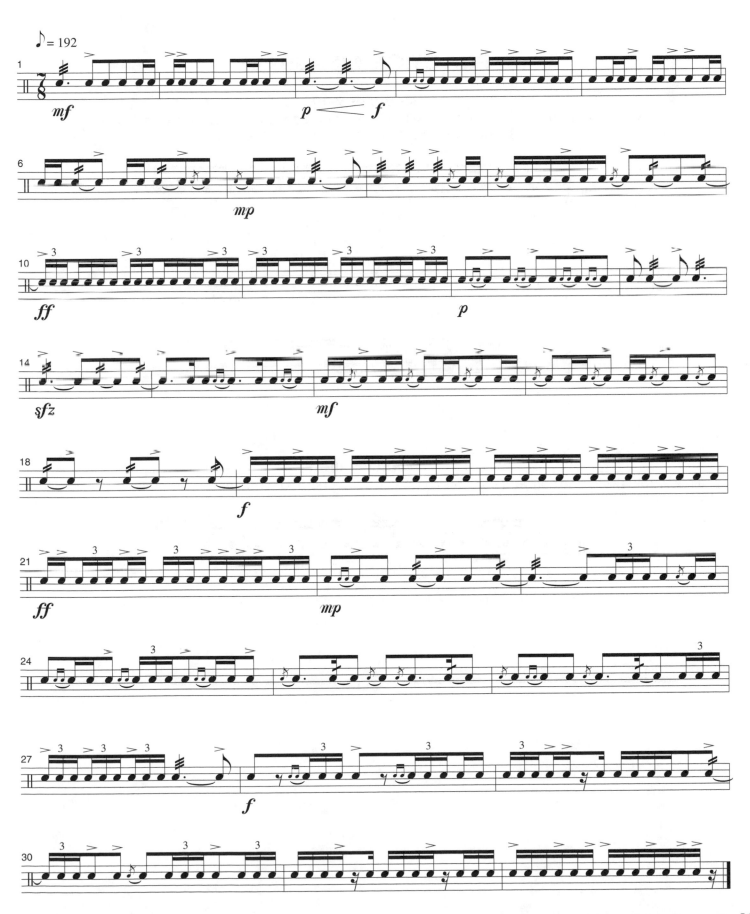

SOLO 8 ANALYSIS

Here's another 2/4 solo in the marching band/drum corps idiom. Rapid interplay between 16th notes and triplets in the latter half of this solo call for precision and stick control. The short rolls add to the intricacies of this piece. Take your time with this one.

PRACTICE MEASURES

Measures 9–10

This across-the-barline flam pattern with a *crescendo* occurs again in measures 13 and 14. Be sure to master it before attempting the solo.

Measures 34–35

Short rolls weaved in among 16th notes appear often here, and in other solos in this book. Try to develop a smooth, natural feel for this pattern.

Measures 40–41

Triplets, 16th notes, and offbeat accents all work together here to produce an interesting rhythmic effect.

SOLO 8

SOLO 9 ANALYSIS

This piece at M.M. = 69 should be played with a "one" feel, similar to Solo 2 in 3/8. The wide use of drags, flams, accents, and rolls make this solo somewhat more difficult than the one on page 9.

PRACTICE MEASURES

Measures 19–20
Single or double sticking may be used in this two-bar phrase.

Measures 37–40
The combination of flams and accents here might present a technical problem. Study this four-bar passage carefully. Also note the wide dynamic changes from one bar to the next.

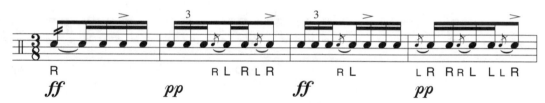

Measures 45–48
The accents in the three-measure triplet pattern below make for an exciting climax to this challenging piece.

SOLO 9

SOLO 10 ANALYSIS

The following thirty-two-measure solo in 4/4 emphasizes long and short rolls, which appear in nearly every bar. Along with the Practice Measures, be especially cautious at measures 7, 19, and 20, all of which incorporate dotted rolls. Be sure you begin and end all rolls on the correct beats.

PRACTICE MEASURES

Measure 13
Short roll patterns and double accents require small changes in stick level and grip pressure.

Measures 16–17
The trick to playing these two measures is maintaining a lower stick level during the rolls and a higher level for the accents. Here again, rapid alteration in grip pressure and stick level is excellent control practice.

Measure 32
In the final measure of Solo 10, in order to establish a feel for the pattern, first try playing the rhythm without the rolls. The rolls and accents may be added afterwards.

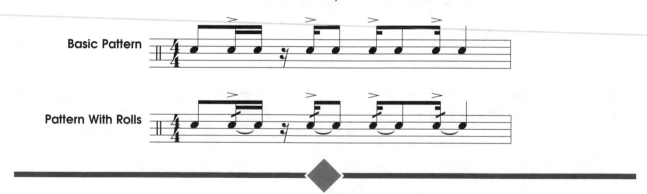

SOLO 10

SOLO 11 ANALYSIS

Solo 11 is built around a theme first stated in the opening four bars. The theme is repeated in measures 5–8, substituting 16th-note triplets, and again in bars 9–12 using 32nd notes. The middle section (measures 13–36) offers an assortment of rolls of varied durations with accents. The final twelve bars are a restatement of the opening theme in reverse.

PRACTICE MEASURES

Measures 11–12
Thirty-second notes with accents on 1 and 4 in measure 11, and on 2 and 5 in bar 12, may require some repeated practice.

Measures 19–20
Be certain that the long rolls in these two bars run for their proper duration, and that the dynamic change from *p* to *mf* is observed.

Measures 31–32
The passage below calls for careful attention to the placement of the short rolls, along with the accents at the end of each roll.

SOLO 11

SOLO 12 ANALYSIS

The following 3/4 solo, at a moderately bright M.M. = 66, mixes 8th notes, triplets, 16th notes, and off-beat accents, all of which give this piece an interesting polyrhythmic texture. Start this solo slower than the suggested tempo, and increase the speed only after all of the figures and accents flow smoothly.

PRACTICE MEASURES

Measures 29–30
The 8th-note rests on the first partial of the triplets require precise timing, particularly at a faster tempo. Work on these two measures slowly if you encounter a problem.

Measures 33–35
Be sure the accented 8th notes stand out strongly over the 16th notes in this three-bar phrase.

Measures 43–44
Note how the accent placement in this two-bar triplet passage suggests a 4/4 ride cymbal beat over the 3/4 pulse.

SOLO 12

SOLO 13 ANALYSIS

This march-oriented 6/8 solo can be played at a brisk 84 b.p.m. It's much easier to think of 6/8 time as a "two beat" pulsation, and to count it in "two." (See below.) Also, be sure there's a noticeable difference between the accented and non-accented notes in this solo.

PRACTICE MEASURES

Measures 21–22
Notice the quarter-note-triplet feel created by the accented flams in these two bars.

R RL   L LR   R RL   L RL   R RL   L LR

Measures 30–31
The drags in this passage need to be executed with clarity. Watch the accents here as well.

(mp) cresc. - - - - - - - - - - - - - - f

Measures 41–42
A nine-stroke roll works best in measure 41, followed by three five-stroke rolls in bar 42.

R - R   L - L   R - R   L - L   R

SOLO 13

SOLO 14 ANALYSIS

Solo 14 in 5/4 is one of the more difficult solos in the book. Beginning and ending with a seven-over-five, accented-16th-note pattern, this piece requires total concentration. Before attempting to play this solo, go through the entire piece and sing the rhythms to yourself. This practice can be very helpful prior to performing *any* new solo.

PRACTICE MEASURES

Measure 1
This seven-over-five pattern, created by the accent placement, also appears in bars 3 and 31.

Measures 10–11
Triplet-partial figures with accents alter the feel of this solo when they appear in bars 10–13.

Measures 25–27
Long rolls tied to 16th-note triplets again call for minute changes in stick pressure.
This three-bar phrase is a sure test of speed and control.

SOLO 14

SOLO 15 ANALYSIS

Odd-time solos can feel extremely awkward at first. Remember that this solo in 7/8 (and others in this book) can be performed slower or faster than the suggested tempo, depending on your individual skills. However, bear in mind that accuracy and clean execution are always more important than speed.

PRACTICE MEASURES

Measures 1–3
These three bars are repeated at the conclusion of the solo, measures 29–31.

Measures 15–16
Though the accent placement appears difficult, if you lead into the first measure with the right hand, all of the accents will fall neatly on the right side.

R L R L R L R L R L R L R L R - R L R L R L R R L R R L

Measures 22–23
The figure consisting of a dotted 16th note followed by a 32nd note is used often in this book. However, this figure can be somewhat more difficult to play in 7/8. Pay careful attention to the *diminuendo* here as well.

ff *dim.* - *p*

SOLO 15

SOLO 16 ANALYSIS

This 3/8 solo is spiced with flams, drags, ratamacues, and accents. One of the secrets to accurate reading is to always read slightly ahead of what you're playing. Once you develop the habit of reading ahead, you'll soon notice a marked improvement in your overall accuracy. Experiment with it here.

PRACTICE MEASURES

Measures 27–28
Try both of the stickings shown below. Use the one that feels most comfortable and natural to you.

Measures 36–39
There's a strong emphasis on rudimental stickings in the four bars below. Note the flam accent in bar 36, the flam tap in measure 37, and the single ratamacues in bars 38 and 39.

Measures 43–46
Using alternate sticking, the accents in this concluding phrase will move from hand to hand. The gradual *crescendo* is also very important here.

SOLO 16

SOLO 17 ANALYSIS

This forty-eight-bar solo has several interesting motifs, the first of which appears in measures 13–16. There are two others at bars 21–24 and 41–44. (See the Practice Measures below.) With the exception of the accents, stick levels should be kept relatively low to maintain the bright M.M. = 116 tempo.

PRACTICE MEASURES

Measures 13–16
Seven-stroke rolls with accents on the first stroke will work in bars 13 and 15.

Measures 21–24
The accented flams in this four-bar phrase offer a lively, syncopated feel.

Measures 41–44
Here's another across-the-barline pattern colored with drags and accents.
Practice this passage slower than M.M. = 116 for starters.

SOLO 17

SOLO 18 ANALYSIS

The following solo takes us through several different time signatures. Beginning in 12/8, the solo also incorporates 7/8 and 5/8 sections. Maintain a steady, even flow as you move from one meter to the next. Careful attention to the accents is also of extreme importance here.

PRACTICE MEASURES

Measures 7–8
The 16th-note rests and accents add to the odd-time feel of this two-bar phrase.

Measures 13–14
The 32nd notes in this 5/8 section should be played softer to achieve a sharp contrast with the accents.

Measure 26
Accented flams on every third 16th note gives this 7/8 measure another across-the-barline feeling.

SOLO 18

SOLO 19 ANALYSIS

Solo 19 begins and ends in 4/4, while the middle section alternates between 2/4, 3/4, and 5/4. Since the quarter note gets one beat throughout this solo, you may choose to simply ignore the changing top number of the time signature and play through the solo as if there were no barlines at all.

PRACTICE MEASURES

Measures 7–9

Drags amidst a syncopated pattern offer a change from a march feel to more of a jazz phrasing.

Measures 25–27

The accented flams in this three-bar passage need to fall into place naturally. Also, note the *crescendo* from *pp* to *ff*.

Measures 32–33

This two-bar section moves from 5/4 to 2/4. The accented flams and rests in both measures may cause a problem. Adding somewhat to the complexity is the *diminuendo* from *ff* to *p*.

SOLO 19

SOLO 20 ANALYSIS

This solo in 7/8 has sections in 3/8, 5/8, and 6/8. You'll also note many 32nd-note figures, along with triplets, drags, flams, and rolls. And notice the time signature changes in every bar between measure 22 and 25. Solo 20 is one of the more advanced solos in this book, so take your time with it.

PRACTICE MEASURES

Measures 10–11
A string of 32nd-note figures in 7/8 and 5/8, with accents, requires clean execution and a careful eye.

Measures 13–14
The accented notes in bar 13 should stand out clearly over the non-accented ones.

Measures 27–28
The two bars below present a mixture of dotted 16ths, triplets, rolls, and accents.

SOLO 20

SOLO 21 ANALYSIS

Here's another forty-eight-bar solo in 5/8. This one is slightly more intricate than the one on page 27, though. The brighter suggested tempo is also a factor here, so allow ample time to master the Practice Measures below before attempting the solo.

PRACTICE MEASURES

Measure 13
Note that this bar consists of a flam accent and a flam tap.

RL R LLR L RRL LLR R
LR L RRL R LLR RRL L

Measures 35–36
The triplet accents in these two bars will fall on alternate hands, assuming you use single sticking throughout. Be sure the left-hand accents are equal in volume to the right, and note the *crescendo* here as well.

LLR L RL RL RLRLR L RLRL RL RLRLR L

mp *cresc.* — *f*

Measures 46–48
Here again, focus on playing the rolls softer than the accented 16th notes in the first two measures to achieve a definite contrast between them.

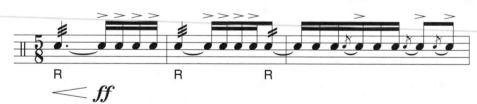

R   R   R

< *ff*

SOLO 21

SOLO 22 ANALYSIS

Solo 22 is a forty-eight-bar piece in 3/4 time. Though this solo doesn't present any particularly difficult challenges, you may still prefer to begin slower than M.M. = 132. As usual, work through the Practice Measures before attempting the entire solo.

PRACTICE MEASURES

Measures 11–12
The five-stroke rolls in these two bars can be played open or closed.

Measures 29–32
Watch the accents in measures 29 and 30, as well as the close drag and flam placement in bars 31 and 32.

Measures 41–42
Back-to-back accents should flow smoothly and be comparable in volume.

SOLO 22

SOLO 23 ANALYSIS

The following solo is another marching-style 6/8. Again, it's usually much easier to count up-tempo 6/8 pieces in "two." Along with the flam taps, accents, and drags, this forty-eight-bar solo makes extensive use of five-, nine-, and thirteen-stroke rolls.

PRACTICE MEASURES

Measures 9–11

The three-bar passage below uses each of the rolls mentioned earlier: the nine-stroke roll in bar 9, the thirteen-stroke in bar 10, and the five-stroke roll in measure 11.

Measures 29–30

Measure 29 consists of flam taps in 6/8. Either an open or closed five-stroke roll is appropriate for bar 30.

Measures 45–46

Here we have two basic measures enhanced with accents, flams, and a five-stroke roll.

SOLO 23

SOLO 24 ANALYSIS

The suggested tempo of M.M. = 200 is quite fast for this solo. As mentioned earlier, a key secret to accurate reading is to keep the eye slightly ahead of the hand at all times. Practice this 5/4 solo at a slower tempo at first, and keep your eyes around one-half to one full bar ahead of your hands. This technique will become easier with consistent practice.

PRACTICE MEASURES

Measures 13–14
The accented drags in these two bars add extra interest to the rhythmic pattern.

Measure 18
In an attempt to keep all but one of the accents on the right side, note the suggested sticking below.
Left-handed players can reverse this.

Measures 25–27
The accented flams in the first two bars of this passage suggest a four-over-five feel.
The *crescendo* from *p* to *mf* adds dynamic interest. Alternate sticking should work best here.

SOLO 24

SOLO 25 ANALYSIS

Solo 25 is an up-tempo 4/4 piece with syncopated rhythmic figures and accents. To obtain an authentic "swing" feel, play all of the 8th notes with a jazz conception. You can also try playing all the accents as rimshots to further enhance the swing flavor of this solo.

PRACTICE MEASURES

Measures 9–10

Accents among jazz–concepted 8th notes give this solo a feel reminiscent of the drumming of the swing era. The two bars below are a good example.

Measures 23–24

Another across-the-barline phrase here may require some extra attention.

Measures 29–30

Note how the accents occur on alternate hands when they're placed on the third partial of each triplet. Practice this two-bar pattern repeatedly until the sticking feels comfortable.

SOLO 25

SOLO 26 ANALYSIS

This basic 3/8 solo has a few tricky spots. Along with the Practice Measures below, watch out for bars 5–8, 29–32, and the last four bars of the solo, all of which may cause problems at a faster tempo.

PRACTICE MEASURES

Measures 1–3
The solo leads off with a series of drags and flam taps, and a single ratamacue in the second bar.

LLRLLRRRLL LRLLRLRL LLRLLRRRLL

Measures 11–12
These 32nd notes surrounded by accents need to be executed as precisely as possible.

Measures 37–40
This four-bar phrase has accented seven-stroke rolls between 16th-note triplets. Several sticking options will work here. For the best effect, the *crescendo* from *p* to *ff* and the *diminuendo* from *ff* to *p* should be carefully observed.

RLRLRLR - LRLR - LRL R - LRLR - LRLRLRL
p cresc. - - - - - - - - - - - - - - *ff* dim. - - - - - - - - - - - - *p*

SOLO 26

SOLO 27 ANALYSIS

Solo 27, in 2/4, makes wide use of flams, 32nd notes, short rolls, and offbeat accents, all of which give this piece a strong drum corps flavor. Careful attention to sticking is important here.

PRACTICE MEASURES

Measures 13–14
Once again, a rapid change in stick height and grip pressure is required for a good balance between the accents and the rolls, particularly in the first of the two bars below.

Measures 21–23
If you lead with the right hand, the accents will naturally go from hand to hand in these three bars.

Measures 41–43
Note the three choices of sticking here: single, double, and paradiddle.

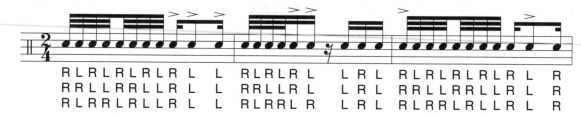

SOLO 27

SOLO 28 ANALYSIS

Pay careful attention to the changing time signatures in the following solo. Beginning in 9/8, the meter changes to 12/8 at bar 13 and moves back quickly to 9/8 in bar 15. A brief 6/8 passage starts at measure 22, with a return to 9/8 at bar 25 to end the solo. Try to keep the transitions between time signatures smooth and even.

PRACTICE MEASURES

Measures 10–11
Both of these measures contain accented press rolls. Also, be sure to catch the accent on the third partial of the triplet in the first bar.

Measures 20–21
The accent pattern in both of these measures produces an interesting effect.

Measures 27–28
Several sticking options exist here. Note two possible choices below, one using single sticking and the other double sticking.

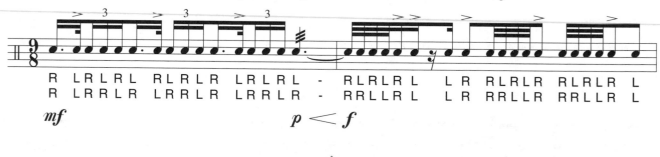

SOLO 28

SOLO 29 ANALYSIS

Solo 29 reverts back to common time, but don't overlook the technical complexities presented here. This solo can be played at M.M. = 104 or faster. Just be certain you've gained control over the more difficult sections before attempting a faster tempo.

PRACTICE MEASURES

Measures 7–9
These three bars place heavy emphasis on the press roll, which needs to be clearly articulated.

Measures 25–26
Dotted 16th notes and accented five-stroke rolls may call for a little additional attention.

Measures 28–29
The accents in the first bar create a very rhythmic effect. The second bar requires two five-stroke rolls, with a nine-stroke roll on the fourth beat.

SOLO 29

SOLO 30 ANALYSIS

Though this solo in 5/8 can be counted in five, it's often easier to count in smaller subdivisions: 1,2,3; 1,2 or 1,2; 1,2,3. Take note of the first two bars of this solo, where bar 1 can be counted 1,2,3; 1,2, and bar 2 as 1,2; 1,2,3.

PRACTICE MEASURES

Measures 22–24
This phrase needs to be counted out carefully, and the dynamic marking carefully noted.

Measures 27–30
Take your time with this passage of long and short rolls, some of which extend over barlines. Note the subtle dynamics beneath the rolls in the first three bars of this section as well.

Measures 41–44
Measures 41 and 42 call for accurate timing of the accented afterbeats, while bars 43 and 44 include accents on the third partial of every triplet.

SOLO 30

SOLO 31 ANALYSIS

Solo 31 is another test of your ability to move between several different time signatures. Starting in 3/4, the change to 2/4 and then to 5/4 abruptly shifts the feeling of this solo. The meter changes occur even more frequently in the latter part of the solo.

PRACTICE MEASURES

Measures 13–15
Accents on the "ah" give this three-bar passage a sense of forward momentum.

Measures 23–24
Eighth-note triplets and triplet partials during the middle section offer a strong change in the feel of this solo.

Measures 29–30
There's a big difference between these two rhythms:

They run close together in the two bars below:

SOLO 31

SOLO 32 ANALYSIS

This next solo offers many of the figures that makes 6/8 such a challenging time signature to play in. The interplay between rudiments, long and short rolls, and odd-accent placement combine to make this a solo that will need a good amount of practice.

PRACTICE MEASURES

Measures 21–24

Note the interesting rhythmic pattern created by the accented flams in this four-bar section. Also notice the four-over-six feel brought out by the flam accents in measure 23.

Measures 26–27

Here again, it's the accents and dynamics that help give these two bars their rhythmic interest.

Measures 42–44

The string of 32nd-note figures must be played with precise clarity. Single or double sticking can be used here, so try them both. Careful control of the *diminuendo* from *ff* to *pp* is also essential.

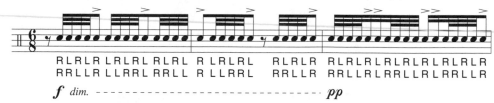

SOLO 32

SOLO 33 ANALYSIS

The following 2/4 solo also has a strong syncopated feel. The 32nd notes with accents and short 16th-note rolls offer an opportunity to really fine-tune your technical ability.

PRACTICE MEASURES

Measures 13–14
Be sure the accents stand out strongly in the 32nd-note passage below.

RLRLR LRLRL RLRL RLRLR LRLRLRL R
RRLLR LLRRL RRLL RRLLR LLRRLLR L

ff

Measures 19–20
Closed five-stroke rolls work in these two measures. Note the two sticking options: one leading with all rights and the other with alternate-hand leads.

R R R R R
R L R L R

mp cresc. - *f*

Measures 33–35
There's a lot of interplay between flams, accents, and short rolls here, with the accent on the first stroke.

L R R   R   L R R L L R   R L R   R   L R R L L R   R L R   R   R   R

mf cresc. - - - - - - - - - - - - - *f* - - - - - - - - - - - - - - *ff* - - - - - - - - -

SOLO 33

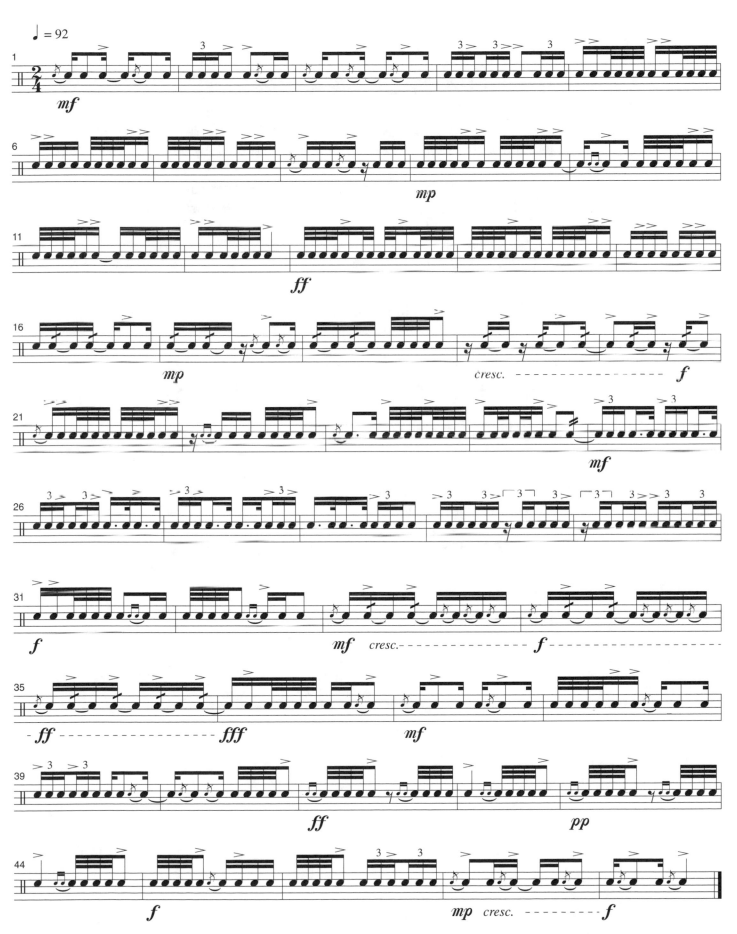

SOLO 34 ANALYSIS

This next solo alternates between 3/8, 5/8, and 6/8. The odd-time 5/8 passages will always feel somewhat awkward compared to the 3/8 and 6/8 sections, but they should feel more natural after a few playings.

PRACTICE MEASURES

Measures 18–20
These three bars in 3/8 tend to suggest a 4/4 "shuffle" rhythm.

Measures 39–40
It's easy to lose the feel of 5/8 here due to the accent placement over the triplets in the first bar.

Measures 44–46
The accents in this passage may present an execution challenge. Two choices of sticking are shown below.

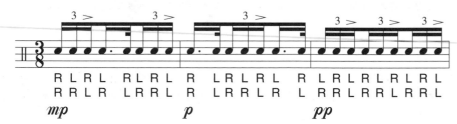

RLRL   RLRL   R   LRLRL   R LRLRLRLRL
RRLR   LRRLR   R   LRRLR   L RRLRRLRRL

mp   *p*   *pp*

SOLO 34

SOLO 35 ANALYSIS

Solo 35 begins in 5/4, changes to 3/4 at bar 8, and returns to 5/4 at measure 13. Another 3/4 section starts at bar 23, with a return to 5/4 at measure 28 to conclude the solo. You should have developed a good feel for playing in "five" by this point in the book.

PRACTICE MEASURES

Measure 5
Note the groupings of "five" on the first and fourth beats of this measure.
Be sure they're spaced evenly and correctly.

Measures 14–15
Here again, it's the accents that make these two bars so much more rhythmically effective.

Measure 28
Work on this measure separately until you're certain it's being played correctly.

SOLO 35

SOLO 36 ANALYSIS

Solo 36 is in 6/8, with two sections of 3/8 in bars 14–20 and 39–42. This solo contains more than its fair share of interesting figures and difficult phrases. Strive for accuracy and technical perfection throughout.

PRACTICE MEASURES

Measures 25–27

The dotted-16th-note figure in 6/8 should feel pretty natural by this point.
Notice the four-over-six feel that occurs from the end of bar 26 through measure 27.

Measures 35–37

Watch the accented and non-accented notes in the first two bars of the following three-bar passage.
Single or double sticking can be used in measure 37.

Measures 43–46

A combination of five-stroke rolls, with accents that fall at the start and end of the rolls,
may require some special attention.

SOLO 36

SOLO 37 ANALYSIS

The following solo includes 16th notes, triplets, long and short rolls, groupings of fives and sevens, accents, drags, and flams. You're likely to find this 4/4 solo a true test of your endurance, stick control, and reading skill. Many sections of this solo present a real technical challenge, so don't be in too much of a rush to play it at top speed. Focus on accuracy and clean execution.

PRACTICE MEASURES

Measures 17–18
Practice this passage slowly at first. Count out loud if necessary, and be certain the accents are placed correctly within the *p* to *f* crescendo.

Measure 22
This measure contains a seven grouping and a five grouping alternated with 8th-note triplets. Odd groupings can be quite tricky. Be sure to space all of the figures accurately.

Measures 26–27
The following two-bar pattern requires speed and precise definition. Be especially careful at the second bar, and strive for an even flow. Either single or double sticking can be used here.

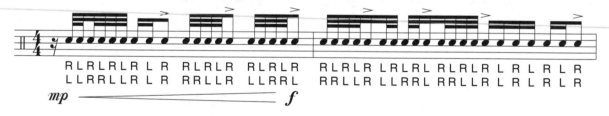

SOLO 37

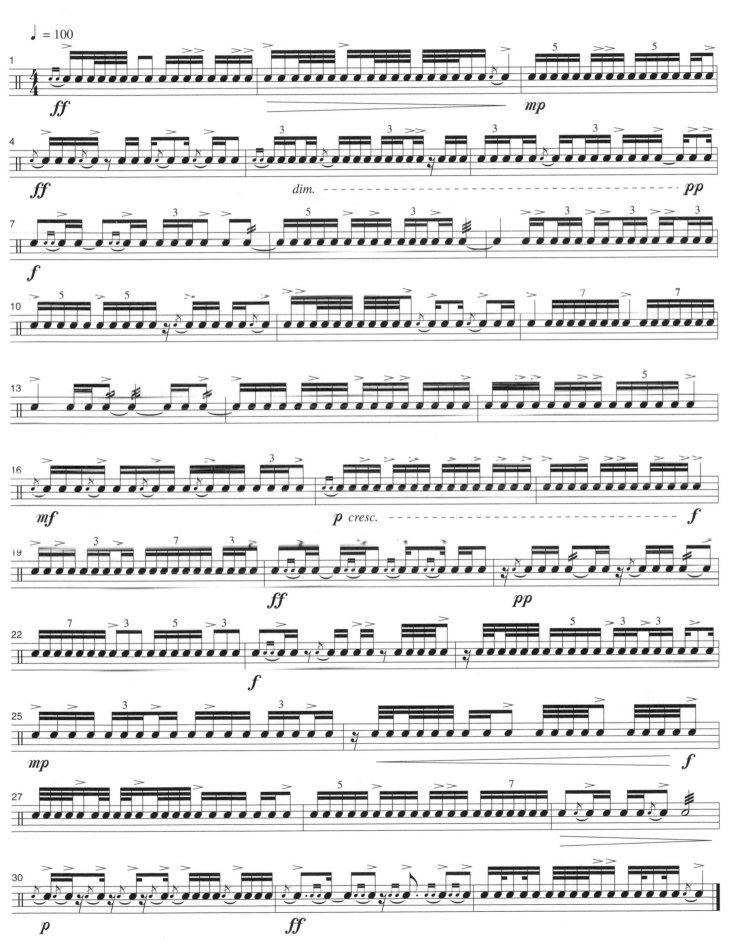

SOLO 38 ANALYSIS

Our final solo is in 12/8. Everything from the sticking, rolls, flams, and accent placement to a wide mixture of figures needs to be watched here. Work through the Practice Measures before attempting this challenging piece.

PRACTICE MEASURES

Measures 12–13
Accurate execution of the accents on the third partial of the triplets in bar 12 is important, as are the triplet flams and short rolls in measure 13.

Measures 21–22
A tight mix of flams and drags leading into 16th notes requires good control. Work these two bars carefully.

Measures 31–32
Both measures below—particularly bar 32—need to be articulated with laser-like precision. Strive for a good balance between the accented and non-accented notes in this two-bar climax.

SOLO 38